I0459356

Grief Mountain

The Calm and Color Trailbook

Amanda Bourque

Also by Amanda Bourque

The "Grief Mountain" Series:
Grief Mountain: A Navigational Guide to Loss
Grief Mountain: The Companion Guide

Other Books:
Living in My Sister's Shadow

Visit www.soberandbeyond for more books and free resources.

Copyright © 2026 by Amanda Bourque
All rights reserved.

No part of this publication may be reproduced, distributed, or transmitted in any form or by any means. Electronic, mechanical, photocopying, recording, or otherwise without prior written permission from the publisher, except in the case of brief quotations used in reviews or articles.

This coloring book contains illustrations created and assembled using licensed design elements and graphics from Canva. All Canva content is used in accordance with Canva's Content License Agreement. Ownership of these elements remains with the original creators, and this book does not claim ownership of any Canva-sourced images or design components.

Every effort has been made to ensure proper use of licensed materials. For questions regarding permissions or usage, please contact: amanda@soberandbeyond.com

ISBN: 979-8-9921861-7-8 (The Calm and Color Trailbook)
ISBN: 979-8-9921861-3-0 (Grief Mountain: Paperback)
ISBN: 979-8-9921861-4-7 (Grief Mountain: Hardcover)
ISBN: 979-8-9921861-5-4 (Grief Mountain: E-book)
ISBN: 979-8-9921861-6-1 (The Companion Guide)

First printing edition 2026
Sober and Beyond
Tampa, FL
www.soberandbeyond.com

Introduction

Grief changes the landscape of our lives. Suddenly familiar paths feel foreign, and every step can feel heavier than the one before. Grief Mountain: The Calm and Color Trailbook was created to walk beside you through this difficult terrain. As part of our grief-support series, this coloring book invites you to slow down, breathe deeply, and rediscover moments of steadiness and connection, one page at a time.

Within these pages, you'll journey along winding trails, quiet forest clearings, mountain overlooks, and sunlit meadows. Each illustration inspired by the healing power of nature and the grounding rhythm of putting one foot in front of the other. Whether you're an experienced hiker or someone who simply finds comfort in the outdoors, these scenes offer a gentle place to rest, reflect, and release what weighs on your heart.

Every line is drawn with intention. To hold space for your memories, your emotions, and your own pace of healing. Here, you are invited to rediscover beauty even in the shadowed valleys and to let color become a path toward calm, clarity, and hope.

Take your time. There is no right way to grieve, and no wrong way to color. This is your journey and you don't have to walk it alone.

Check out the other books in the Grief Mountain series:

Grief Mountain: A navigational Guide to Loss

Grief Mountain: The Companion Guide

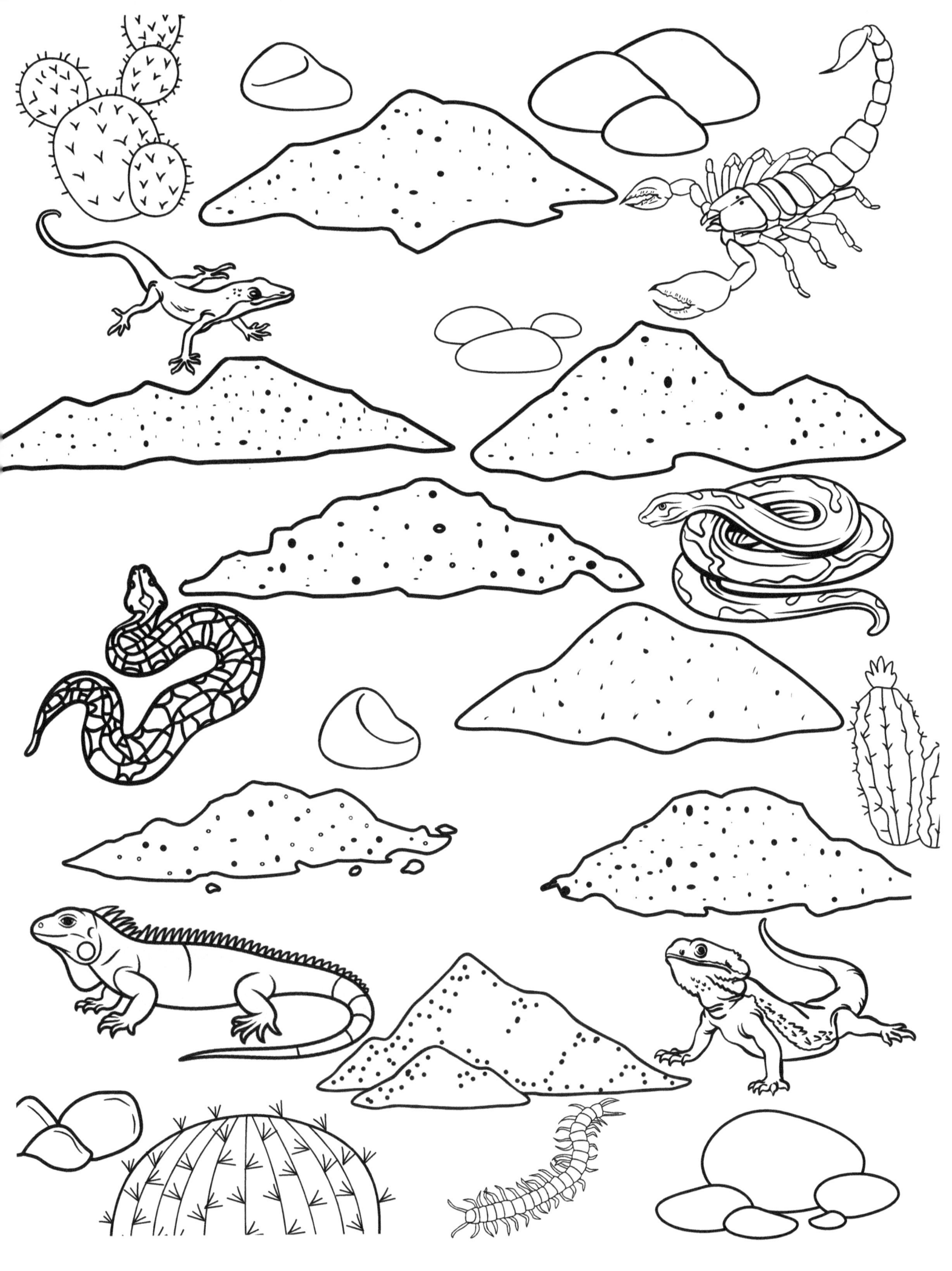

"I would recognize you in total darkness, were you mute and I deaf. I would recognize you in another lifetime entirely, in different bodies, different times. And I would love you in all of this, until the very last star in the sky burnt out into oblivion."

Madeline Miller, *The Song of Achilles*

About the Author

Amanda Bourque is a certified addiction recovery coach and certified life coach who combines these unique skill sets to support people who suffer from addiction with an emphasis on their family and loved ones. Grief Mountain is Amanda's second publication following her debut memoir Living in My Sister's Shadow chronicling her and her sister's true-life stories.

After studying business management at Southern New Hampshire University and graduating summa cum laude, she founded her own addiction recovery coaching service, Sober and Beyond, in honor of her beloved sister, Jenna. Amanda also frequently volunteers at an addiction rehabilitation center, which has helped her better understand her addicts' struggles and mindsets making her a more effective resource for their recovery journeys.

After enduring many personal ordeals, Amanda is now determined to live her life to the fullest and help others along the way. She has pursued her passion for travel all her adult life and even spent five years living overseas, including in India, her favorite destination. She loves planning her next adventure abroad, reconnecting with nature, and taking annual hiking trips in Utah. She currently resides in Tampa, Florida.

For more information about Amanda, her mission, and overcoming addiction, please visit her website at: www.soberandbeyond.com

www.ingramcontent.com/pod-product-compliance
Lightning Source LLC
Chambersburg PA
CBHW041518120626
46551CB00018B/2485